Stardust and Ruins

Alistair J. Kraft

Thanks to Anya Anne Light for publishing 'Co-Evolve.'

Many of these poems can be found in some form on Medium.com

Cover designed by Merel Pierce

Formatting by Alistair J. Kraft

Internal images found at Wikimedia Commons:

Front image: Embroidery pattern with seven six-pointed stars and four corner pieces

Chapter headers: Starburst fresco, Villa Romana del Casale, Piazza Armerina, Italy

Contents

Introduction

The bulk of these poems were written between 2020 and 2022. The exceptions were written years back and held onto because I loved them more than anything else I'd ever written and wanted to save them for a collection worthy of them. This collection is it. Without question, this collection contains the best writing I have ever done. All it took was a great deal of emotional pain which a reader can see me working through in the text. Oddly enough, it seems to have been more effective than therapy as the creative process of this book has left me feeling more settled in myself than I've ever been.

I'm so thankful I can take this collection out of my wounded places and put it on pages to share. It's been very freeing, and makes me excited to see how my writing will evolve moving forward.

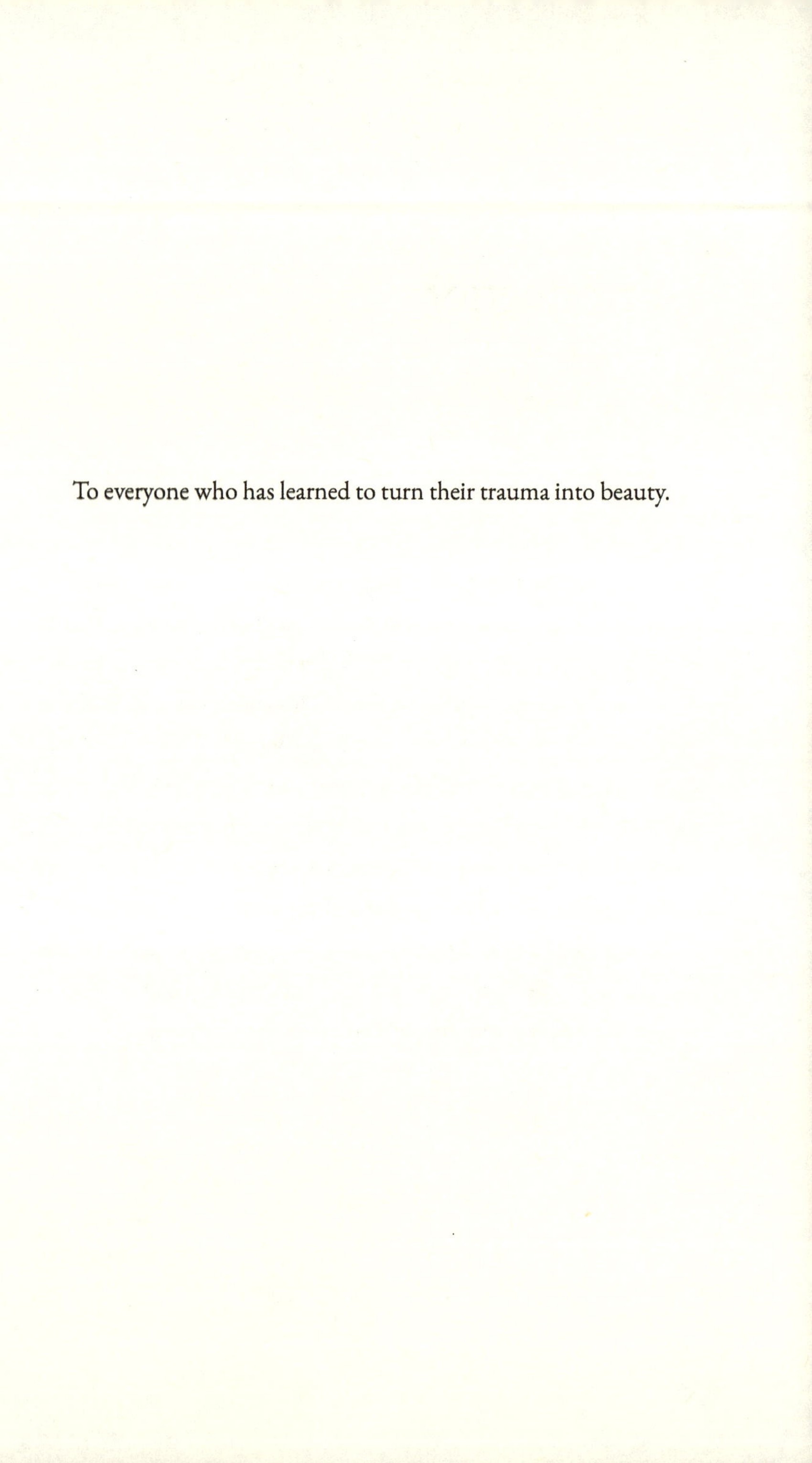

To everyone who has learned to turn their trauma into beauty.

'All bad poetry springs from genuine feeling.'
~ Oscar Wilde

'There is no greater agony than bearing an untold
story inside you.'
~ Maya Angelou

If All of Time Happens Concurrently

If all of time happens concurrently,
then is it true that I'm existing

still

in that moment

I often think is just a loop in my memory

of first seeing your feet under that room divider,

then the smile of recognition that lit up your face

so bright, pure happiness—

when we first saw each other in this lifetime.

Does that moment still exist for some version of me?

Do you visit it too?

The coffee never cooling, the conversations

around us never winding down, an eternal

first date, suspended in repeated gestures,

your eyes averted, your hands

shaking, longing to reach out and

connect

for the first time.

Is that why the space in my ribs is so hollow, because it contains

the world where that moment plays over and

over, and what of me that I carried there

recognized what of you that you carried

beside your heart, and if I crack

my ribs open can I climb in,

go back to that

coffee-sunsweet

moment and bind my chest so tightly

that the essential heart of me can't

leap out, allowing itself to

die?

In that moment, frozen, we hovered before the

crash.

A Study in Grief

My life has been a study
    in grief
    and how to obscure it.

"You play your cards close to your chest,"
my uncle remarked once, and I was
delighted
at being seen
so clearly.

Seen in my not being seen.
A deer in the woods.
A mouse in the meadow.
Hiding,
so no fierce hunger could sniff out
the wounded leg marking me
easy prey.

I walked boldly into traps anyway,
when a human held out a hand,
palm open,
offering binding.

Antiseptic is supposed to hurt, after all —
that's how you know it's working.

Escape cost me blood,
limbs gnawed off.

The wounds are there, open,
gaping,
needing treatment but hidden under
tight wrapping. I've learned
to move around my injuries,
almost never let my limp slip through.

My shields are in place as I move
through the world, very, very
carefully, offering
only barest glimpses underneath.

I'm still learning what gentleness feels like.

I'm learning that help doesn't have to hurt —
gentle hands, clean water,
offerings of food,
are better for healing than
sharp antiseptic.

The Hollow Still Rattles

The initial grieving and sharp hollowing pain of the loss
— you, once promising forever,
the faith that you meant it,
days in the kitchen making lemongrass jam, planning a garden
we know we won't manage to save from squirrels,
sitting quietly together with our books,
you sketching, long legs crossed at the ankle,
my fingers scribbling wild thoughts, spinning webs, looking up
only to share a soft smile,
a feeling of home I've never had anywhere else—
finally
healed enough that I dared to look
inward, assess the damage.
There are fundamental organs —
heart, lungs, trust,
missing
from inside of me, and I picture them
discarded (brutal, cold, indifferent)
on the side of the highway to Colorado,
not even resold, or consumed,
but just unwanted detritus.
The depth of the waste shocks me as much as the suddenness

of your words, "No, I can't do this anymore."
We had always talked about the romance of our corpses
rotting together, compost for flowers, food for the animals,
skeletons collapsing into each other.
You didn't even feed my heart to your dog.
Then I may still have slept at your feet.
Years later the hollow in me still rattles when someone tries
to fill it, offering parts of themselves–
but the transplants
never take — the edges are too scarred. The body rejects
their affection after a short struggle.
Organs that are once removed from a body become
incapable of healing without blood pumping
through them. Our miraculous creation did not account
for this injury, or did not account for a body
surviving it, even when the soul does not.
A body with too much cut away
is incapable of rejuvenating.
It can never return to the original state, the
violence of evisceration
unable
to be hidden.
Stagnant blood floating in darkness is no longer magic.
An apology — to anyone who has tried to love me
the last three years — you deserve
to feel loved like I deserved
to feel love, but we were all
punished for our wishes all the same.
There are more of us out there, walking
hollows — we appear whole from the front until

we turn sideways, and you see

we're concave, skin pulled in

to protect us, but that just reveals

our secret– creatures out of myth that no one wants

to turn into, no one should want

to try to save.

A Chimera of Coping Mechanisms

I'm a chimera of coping mechanisms cobbled
   together to look like a functioning person.
   I wrap tight around the dark places
   that stitch me together
   and refuse to let anyone in the door
   where they might see the shoddy workmanship.

   I have never been so damaged.
   I have never been so honest.

   I like being ruined, broken. I feel
   fulfilled,
   or at least like my destiny is. I always
   knew I'd end up this way, I just
   hadn't realized how much it would hurt
   to get here.

   Or how happy I could be,
   once the journey was over.

   It's so much easier to make peace

with fate,
than to fight it.
Stretching out amidst my wreckage
I gaze out the window, a faint breeze
shifting the curtains over the shadows
and dust
and I think of all the freedoms my solitude
affords me. Nothing to push back against
me when I try to take up space.
I tell myself it's enough. More
than enough.

What other choice do I have, in the end?
Eventually, stitches are no longer necessary.
They break down.
Fall out —
until only faint pale spots are left to mark the trauma.

A Form of Homecoming

My body first learned its boundaries
    when pressed against yours–

    the embrace sacred, a form of homecoming
    as I rested on your chest
    or wrapped around your back and you sighed
    with relief to be there too.

    And I knew every time your fingers brushed my thigh,
    it was seeking reassurance that I was walking
    beside you, and every time our fingers
    twined we were connected so intimately
    it felt indecent to do such a simple thing in public.

    As my body changed and shifted it still fit perfectly
    against yours and so I learned my new shape
    through your hands, your eyes, your rest against me.

    Your desire for me never faltered, the love beyond
    the physical, though undeniably rooted in the flesh as well.

    My darling, it was holding you against my chest

that I first learned how much more tenderly
you can feel love when your chest is flat and you can press
heartbeat to heartbeat.
How vulnerable men must be in their emotions
with such a raw spot, prone to such damage
that it is protected by so much rage.

Now I cradle my small dog, feel his back
press against my breastbone, feel his warm fur,
and deep sleeping breathing, and I love him
more completely than ever before now that my obstructing
costume is removed, the skin still so slightly
puckered and purple, the hair yet sparse.

All this tenderness in the night and I long
to reach out and feel your shoulder, to know my home
is still there, will still sigh when I press against it,
and welcome me in against the heart as if I were
wanted there, and would never have to leave again.

Your Last New Partner

How many partners have said to you what I said
    that afternoon in the kitchen as you washed dishes,
    when it was still new and felt inexplicably
    solid between us? Despite the magic I still felt
    seeing you in the sunshine in my home and smiling
    at me– how many said, 'I don't need to be your only partner,
    as long as I'm your last new partner' and you agreed
    readily, crinkles at the corners of your eyes.

    But I always knew, I think, that the avoidance
    that kept you in multiple relationships wouldn't be resolved
    by my love, no matter how much space my heart
    allowed you to learn and change.

    And I saw through you like the kitchen window
    and you said you'd wanted a partner to truly see you,
    and I did– I did– but you
    weren't ready to be seen that well,
    so you forgot the things I saw, denied
    that I knew, and I became just another link
    in your long chain of lovers (avoidance)--

I'm glad you've come to terms, now.
I hope you can stop hurting people. Maybe
you'll find a new last partner.

I think you were already mine.

Even if I Don't Want You Back

Even if I don't want you
   back, I'm allowed to grieve you.

   And by 'you' I don't mean
   your physical presence, or
   the feeling I had when you reached out
   and brushed your fingers against my thigh.

   'You,' now, is the damage
   that you inflicted on me
   on your chaotic path to find yourself.

   How you only meant for me to be a dalliance,
   and then got caught up, became unsure
   how to free yourself.

   You were curled up
   like a cornered animal who
   sees the exit but fears the run.

   Who wants to be seen, but
   isn't ready to process what being seen

means.

So you lurked in habits like shadows,
whispered "toxic" to yourself while I
spun, wild, confused, for honest footing.

Who could miss harm parading
as a person wearing the guise of love?
Yet we all fall for that mask over and over

as it morphs and sometimes we are the one
wearing it, with scrying lenses that
strip away lies told
to me, lies told
to yourself.

Who would not grieve a wound they'll carry
to death,
the diagnosis terminal —

that may not kill us fast,
or directly, but that will wear us down
until we retreat to our den,
tired, done, dying.

I'll remember you on the brink of my death.
The wound you left not easily mollified
by a new lover.

No risking a matching mark, a second wound.

I'm all scar tissue and solitude and you —

you got to emerge from your chrysalis triumphant and new.

I Could Have Held You Differently

In my mind I picture you now—
huddled against the pillows of
my/our bed, eyes pale
and wide, face somehow thinner
and I can see now how fragile
you were, a thin
coating over glass that had shattered
and you were patching it
inexpertly,
silent in your pain and concentration,
but I could sense the edges
grinding.
    I wish now I could have held you
    differently, reach my arms out and enfold
    you, offer a safe haven to you
    as you did for me
    as your broken pieces reconfigured
    under your skin,
    as you pieced together a new
    internal geometry.
    Mine was always clear,

my inner pieces made of air and
steel, just forcing a way to the surface
when finally I was able to breathe it out.
My darling, we are not the same creature–
I wanted nothing more than to be the
rampart
you built yourself against,
climbing slowly past the debris,
growing for the sun in gentle,
tender shoots.

I'll Carry You Till the End

Each year that has passed has built up the scar tissue —
Another layer till I can't count them anymore. The thickness of it
  keeps
  everything at a remove, even if I wish
  I could pull another in closer.
  Even finding out you've moved on —
  successful, happy, wanted —
  only threw me off for a day before the void moved back in,
  swallowing the scream at the reminder
  that I was always the one who loved more.
  I don't actually remember what being in love felt like —
  I just know that for a time every love song felt like you.
  Now I've lost the translation key, even
  to the heartbreak songs, and all I can feel these days are
  the wistful, wishing for something,
  wishing more that something had never come along.
  Getting over you and healing
  from you are different things. A wound
  always takes longer to heal than the moment of injury.
  I was meant to be a diversion.
  You were meant to be for the rest of my life.
  You're gone, but I'll carry you with me

till the end anyway.

Stitches can't close a wound with no defined edges.

It still hurts, though, to know that I once knew

what love felt like in a glance

across a room. What home felt like

in the brush of a hand.

The sky feels as empty as my chest

The sky feels as empty as my chest.
   No clouds to break up the expanse so wide a bird would
   fall to exhaustion before reaching the edge.
   The tops of trees scratch messages
   into the blank, swaying softly
   with wind, or sorrow.
   I fear it still won't be space enough for
   the scream
   locked in my throat,
   caught on the strong edges
   of my ribs, tethered
   there, unable to escape
   without eviscerating me.

I'm a walking mausoleum

I'm a walking mausoleum
  containing all the parts of me
  that haven't survived.

  I write eulogies for them, call them
  poems when I mean
  laments.

  Ink spreads more easily than marble carves–
  and can't be read by fingertips in the dark.

No expensive funeral for me

No expensive funeral for me, if
  I even have one.
  Fling my body out on the grass
  under open air —
  Crack my chest and force
  it open, exposing
  my heart to blue expanse.
  Ribs outstretched like
  wings
  to guide me back up
  into Vast
  nothing, the opposite of
  angel fall.

The song of nature's rebirth

The song of nature's rebirth
    is heard so clearly in the quiet
    of a cemetery.
    Birdsong in spring under
    weeping willows echoes
    against still marble faces draped
    in dust —
    A reminder that not everything
    comes back.

The sunlight brought me back to you--

For Lao Wen

The sunlight brought me back to you —
    I couldn't see you until I stood
    in the light,
    blocking you into shadow.
    Your hand reached out,
    "You have light on you,"
    you said, and
    your fingers stretched, stroking
    the glow of my outline.
    I ached.
    I have been looking for you for so long —
    of course you found me first.

Embraces from a setting sun

Embraces from a setting sun
  look like long fingers of dark gauze
  stretching from the horizon, to your feet,
  your shoulders,
  creeping up to stroke
  your hair.
  The touch is cool, chilling,
  stark contrast to the sun's kisses
  that heat flesh,
  leaves blushes that we call
  burns.

I Woke Up Thinking of Your Face

The wound I thought so long
   healed that I ceased to guard it,
   imagining it hidden behind scar
   tissue and silence–
   (everyone *knows* if they know enough not to mention it)--
   I thought there was nothing left, not even
   a sour taste, too busy surviving
   bigger, greater traumas
   that shook me just as deeply, that were
   just as cruel, but more violent, more recent,
   and spring came in with a stroll through the cemetery
   and flowers in the air over the restful dead and you
   got in out of nowhere.
   I woke up thinking of your face
   for the first time in fifteen years and
   is your hair still long,
   is your heart still as pure, really,
   as age can make what I believed of your intrinsic goodness?

Co-Evolution

There is a pathway into
    my heart that only you
    are shaped to follow, forged
    by the sum total of our lives,
    experiences, bringing us inexorably
    inevitably
    fatefully to each other's arms we co-
    evolved to fit together with a
    blinding perfection, heart to
    heart, soul to
    soul and from that we both
    find a place to call home, someone
    to touch those places no one else
    is shaped to reach in our depths.
    Of all the possible lovers in a life
    this is your home in my soul, only I
    am this home in yours.

Darwin's Finches

Science and faith are not
   mutually exclusive – there is no
   reason
   to see evolution as a threat to belief–
   Who can look at this
   finch's beak, and see also
   that finch's beak, and the varying
   flowers that nourish them–
   allowing all four species to survive together, a joint
   and genius merger–
   and not feel awe?
   Darwin wasn't a heretic,
   he was a prophet,
   discovering the hand of a maker
   too subtle for much need of
   burning bushes and pillars
   of salt.
   It is wondrous, this ability to be
   miraculous– that is built into our
   very DNA, our forms
   don't need to be guided every
   step

when stardust and magic
created us,
when the adaptable
blueprints for each species,
parts of the larger working,
ticking whole, this
glorious experiment
floating in the vastness,
were built into us,
drafted divinely,
the mechanism to thrive
inspired in the
clay from which
we were formed.

Pieces of Meteor

Pieces of meteor are priced
   clearly on shelves
   with stones, the bones
   of Earth on sale under enticing
   lights. I long to touch the void
   incarnate, brought down to my
   height, feel the grit of eons
   on my fingertips, taste
   the stars and eternity.
   A wallet doesn't expand
   like a heart,
   and why,
   my kin,
   this stardust from which we are
   all
   made,
   why so dear when our own blood
   glistens with the same sacred matter,
   the same infinity?

The Truth of Moon and Stars

They say that aiming for the moon means
    even if you fall short, you'll land
    among the stars– but the moon
    is so much nearer, our hands must
    cover it from view, but that same hand
    obscures galaxies
    far more distant.
    A short leap lands you in treetops
    gazing up at a pocked and pitying face,
    the stars too distant to even feel sorrow
    for your aborted leap, the tragedy
    of human life, the ever failing.
    So they drop hopes to us we can carry
    in our pocket, digging deep in dirt and earth
    will land one more surely
    among the stars than a leap at the moon,
    so close it knows we gaze at it
    with longing and awe.

Selfish in the grass

Selfish in the grass, stars
    in eyes, reflecting
    darkness and edges of galaxies,
    the imagined lines trace the patterns
    of constellations
    known and new and longing
    for one to break loose,
    plummet
    fire across the black–
    shooting wishes.
    Come, Orion,
    loosen your belt. Release a gem
    for my eyes, changing
    forever
    your ancient outline,
    changing everything
    painted in a night sky.

Gold is Not So Precious

Gold is not so precious after all,
    no more precious than stardust,
    hidden everywhere,
    available to all.

    The light reveals it, slanting
    light in evening, trees
    glowing from their hidden stockpile
    released to air and all
    in autumn, the richest hue,
    free as the stardust

    that makes us all.

Fleeing Uranus leaves trails of tears

Fleeing Uranus leaves trails of tears,

   (of semen) on the inky sheets of void,

   of night sky, where his son (who would devour

   his own flesh soon enough) thought

   his adornments looked best. Yet

   they can fall, they do

   fall– and we are all stardust.

   He is the father of all life

   on Earth, even from the void his essence

   flames and falls, impact more painful

   than sensual, and Gaia gives birth

   again and again

   in silent agony, tears in streams

   and oceans,

   her son thwarted,

   her son (twice) fooled.

There is something to the thought

There is something to the thought–
    the scythe that struck Uranus at the root
    of creation now is the symbol
    of death. Because the path to death for us all
    begins at the moment of conception– no one
    condemns us more to the end of our lives
    than our parents who brought us into existence.

Starry Fingers Weave

Starry fingers weave
    into grass, tug
    the roots back exposing
    her neck,
    vulnerable gasp of startlement
    and desire,
    eyes heavy lidded with moss
    and grassy banks waiting. The sky
    falls
    to touching her trees and streams –
    while Saturn lurks
    up the beach,
    scythe in hand to defend his
    ravished mother,
    to put the stars back
    where he thinks they
    belong.

So You Were Raped by an Eagle

Though you can guess at his
     real name, starts with Z, ends
     with –eus, and you're almost
     inevitably with divine child.
     Lucky, at least you can
     pinpoint the culprit, unlike victims of
     Poseidon, who go into the ocean
     virgins, and then find their
     hymens breaking with their water.
     No one will believe you're still
     untouched by mortal man. No one
     believed your aunt about those
     barbarians, either, and she was
     beaten and bloody and spent her
     days unwed, unwanted.
     More fool her for being
     sad about it, really, as what
     good are men anyway? Always
     making you iron their togas and
     clean up their vomit after a
     rousing round of booze orgies.
     Praying to Hera won't help, though she

should be sympathetic, theoretically, considering

her experience of men, of

marriage, but the jealous

old bitch won't be, not that

you asked for it by letting your

hair dry in the sun one day when *He*

happened to be passing. And he won't

offer support. He'll deny everything

until the child proves amazing and then

he may be granted a constellation,

while you watch the night sky and wonder if

you're still beautiful enough to be in

danger. Unless the child is a

girl, in which case her beauty may

start wars, but won't win her any

kindness, from gods or man. Perhaps the

midwife can help you remove the

problem, but you'll have to

lie about the father, if even the

strongest brew can eject a divine

passenger. Word will get around anyway and

you'll be damaged goods for life,

shunned by men, family and

immortals, none believing your

tale save the one most

likely to deny it– and it's

not like he'd speak to mortals

anyway. He'd get his sun son to

lie, too. Who will take pity?

Who will believe your

innocence long enough to

marry you off to a new

master. No, really the eagle

was a blessing in disguise, a

reason to go over that ledge and

free fall,

violating

his element,

as he

did

yours.

The Library of the Mind

The library of the mind
    is lodged in a mezzanine the
    color of all of your favorite words,
    scented with every flower
    you ever received for love.

    Grander than Alexandria yet
    more revered and not
    lost to the centuries, the
    texts grow, spines
    crackling like autumn leaves.

    The copyists are monks,
    their fine wrists
    thin as the bones of birds,
    gentle humming blending
    more glorious than a symphony.

    There are illuminations on
    their bare scalps, like
    brilliant scars, the
    wisdom of ancients,

ingrained and unreadable.

Acknowledgments

I want to offer the most profound and sincere gratitude to the Kickstarter backers, both long term friends and supporters, and people who don't know me but graciously took a chance on a modest poet, who helped me make this book a reality.

One million thanks to: Rebecca Lynn McNair, Jackie Ferguson, Staci Booth, Caleb Monk, Kira Odom, Jim and Jean Kraft, Adriane Zonker, Dustin Riley, Benny L. Wallace II, kirbsmilieu, Doctor Razmataz, Becky Haar, Sandy Reiberg, Selene, Jessica Jackson-Salvucci, Kelly Glover, Elizabeth Moss, Christopher Adkins, Jessica Kraft, Robert Kraft, Angela Silliman-Grosheim, JoAnn Swett, Sidney Grady, and Amy Firestone.

I appreciate the support more than I can express, even as a poet. Thank you.

About Author

Alistair J. Kraft is a Midwestern native who is pretty sure he should have been born in Seattle. Scribbling poetry to process the trauma of being alive since he was very young, he's been gratified to see that the poems have actually gotten worth reading. When he's not gutting himself in ink, he's usually buried under rescue dogs or cats, extoling the virtues of Dungeons and Dragons, writing books under a pseudonym, pretending the 90's still aren't over, and researching more efficient ways to get animal fur off of a largely black wardrobe. He is convinced that his friends are the best people in the world and every day he's grateful for the abundance of beautiful things in his life. Despite the cat fur.

Also By

Books of Poetry

Uncertain Rustling

Assorted Writings can be found:

Alistair J. Kraft on Medium.com

9 798218 067601